Piano • Vocal • Guitar

MY HEART WILL GO ON
(LOVE THEME FROM 'TITANIC')
& 23 MORE SONGS FROM TODAY'S HIT MOVIES

ISBN 0-7935-9605-X

HAL•LEONARD®
CORPORATION
7777 W. BLUEMOUND RD. P.O. BOX 13819 MILWAUKEE, WI 53213

D1597159

Visit Hal Leonard Online at
www.halleonard.com

BEST OF MY LOVE
from BOOGIE NIGHTS

Words and Music by MAURICE WHITE
and AL McKAY

DO YOU REALLY WANT TO HURT ME

from THE WEDDING SINGER

Words and Music by GEORGE O'DOWD, JON MOSS,
MICHAEL CRAIG and ROY HAY

FAIRYTALE
(A True Story)
from the Paramount Motion Picture FAIRYTALE: A TRUE STORY

By ZBIGNIEW PREISNER

Gently

With pedal

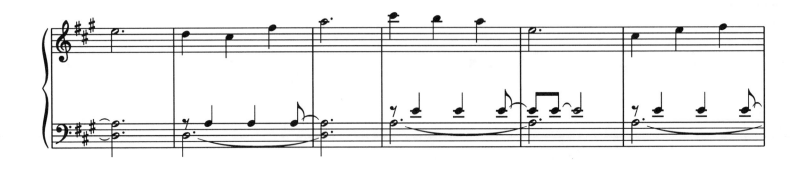

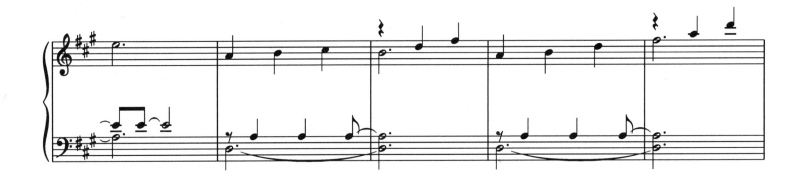

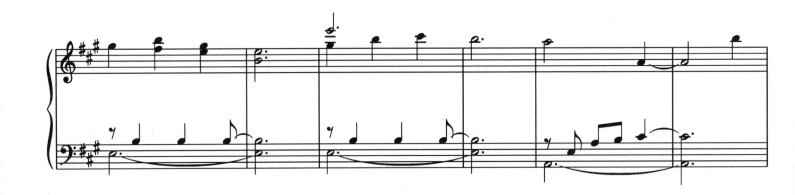

(I Love You)
FOR SENTIMENTAL REASONS
from AS GOOD AS IT GETS

Words by DEEK WATSON
Music by WILLIAM BEST

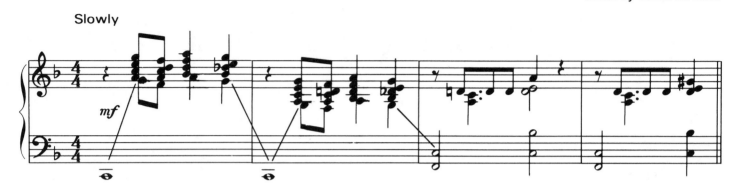

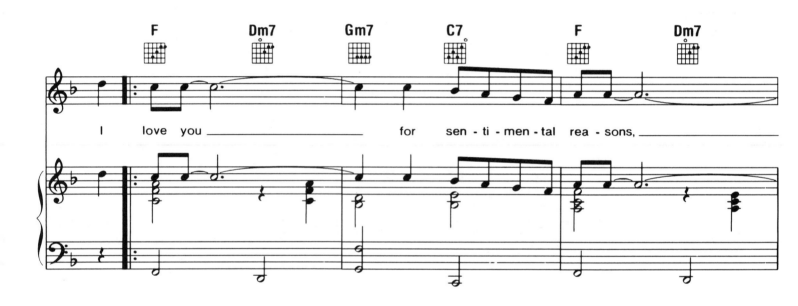

I love you _____ for sen-ti-men-tal rea-sons, _____

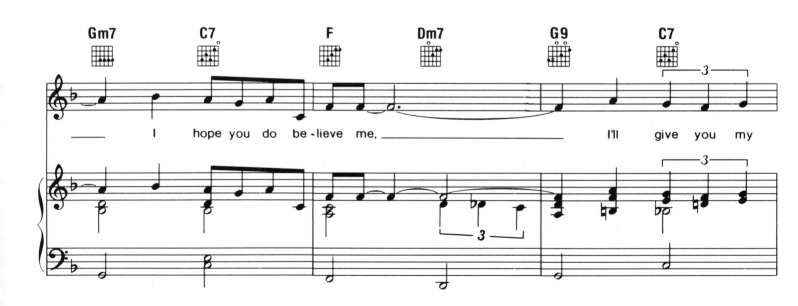

_____ I hope you do be-lieve me, _____ I'll give you my

GO THE DISTANCE

from Walt Disney Pictures' HERCULES

Music by ALAN MENKEN
Lyrics by DAVID ZIPPEL

HOT STUFF
from THE FULL MONTY

Words and Music by PETE BELLOTTE,
HAROLD FALTERMEYER and KEITH FORSEY

Moderate Disco

(Bass simile throughout)

Sit-tin' here eat-in' my heart out wait-in', wait-in' for some lov-er to call.
Look-in' for a lov-er who needs an-oth-er; don't want an-oth-er night on my own.

Dialed a-bout a thou-sand num-bers late-ly. al-most rang the phone off the wall.
Wan-na share my love with a warm-blood-ed lov-er; wan-na bring a wild man back

home. Look-in' for some hot stuff, ba-by, this eve-nin';__ I need some hot stuff, ba-by, to-night.
Got-ta have some hot love,

HIT THE ROAD TO DREAMLAND
from L.A. CONFIDENTIAL

Words by JOHNNY MERCER
Music by HAROLD ARLEN

*Chord Names For Guitar

28

HOLD ME NOW

from THE WEDDING SINGER

Words and Music by TOM BAILEY,
ALANNAH CURRIE and JOE LEEWAY

I BELIEVE IN YOU AND ME

from the Touchstone Motion Picture THE PREACHER'S WIFE

Words and Music by DAVID WOLFERT
and SANDY LINZER

I SAY A LITTLE PRAYER

featured in the Tri-Star Motion Picture MY BEST FRIEND'S WEDDING

Lyric by HAL DAVID
Music by BURT BACHARACH

THE ODD COUPLE II
Theme from Neil Simon's THE ODD COUPLE II

Written by ALAN SILVESTRI

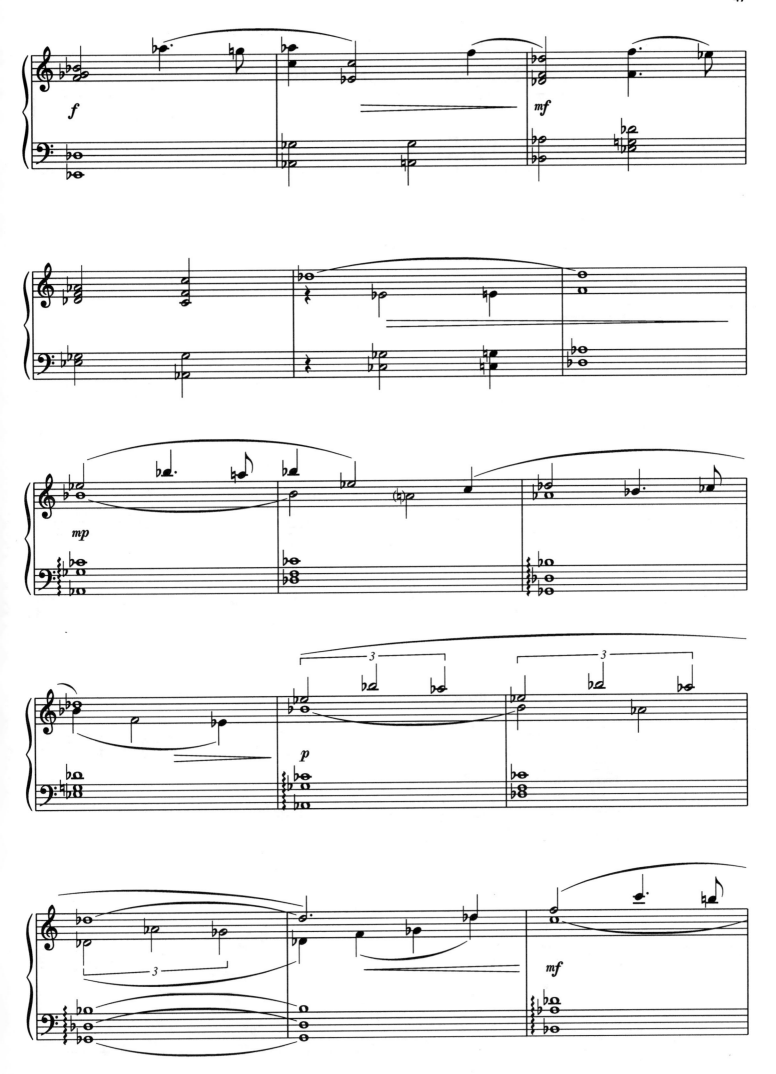

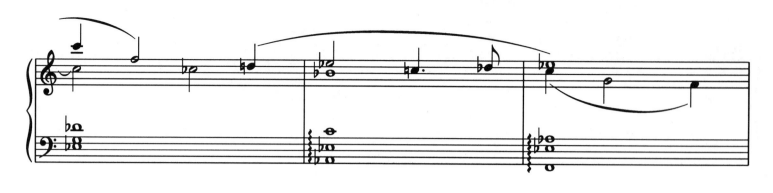

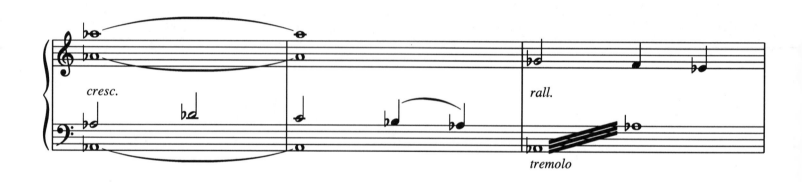

Broadly, slightly slower

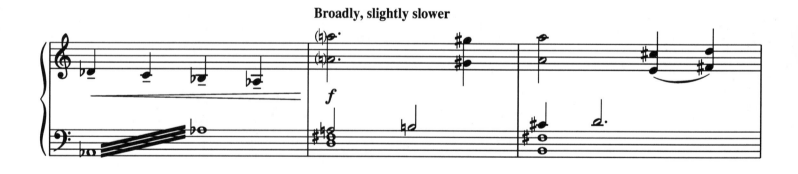

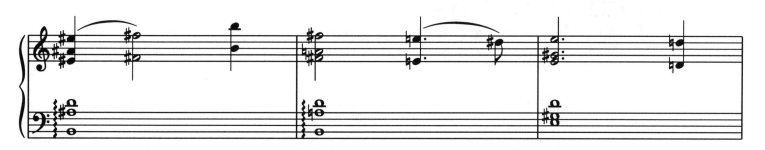

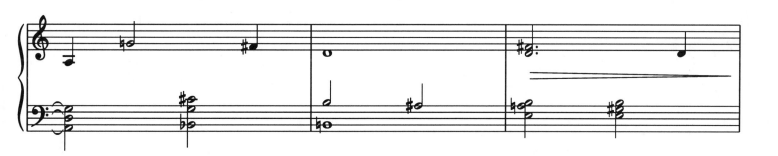

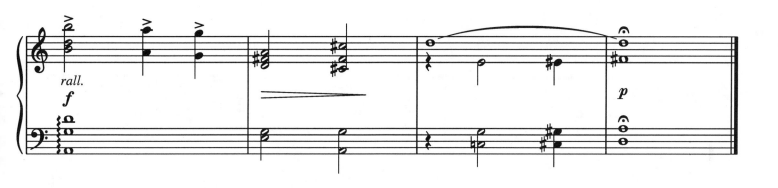

THE MAN IN THE IRON MASK

from the United Artists Motion Picture THE MAN IN THE IRON MASK

By NICK GLENNIE-SMITH

Slow

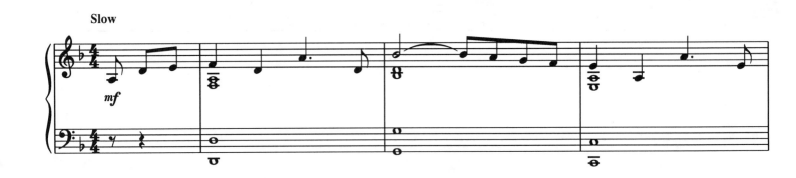

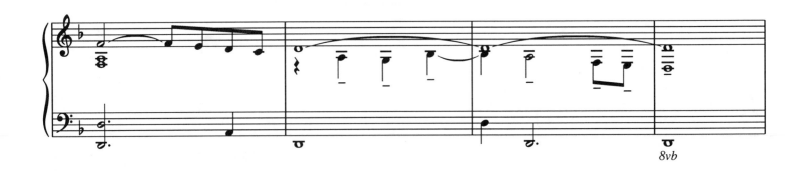

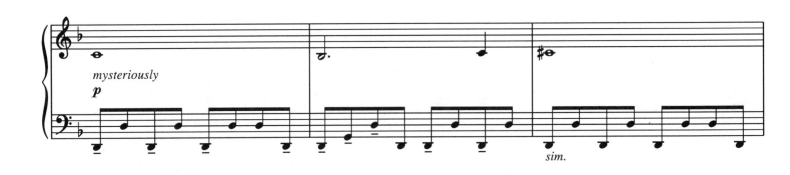

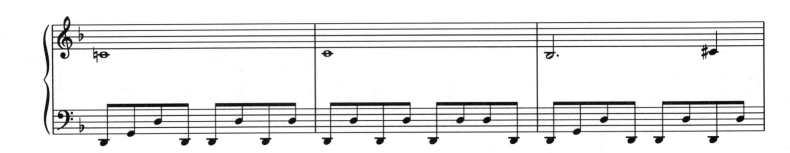

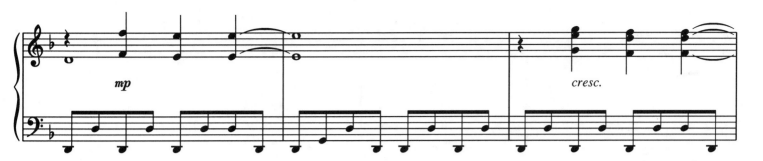

Slow 2, with a beat

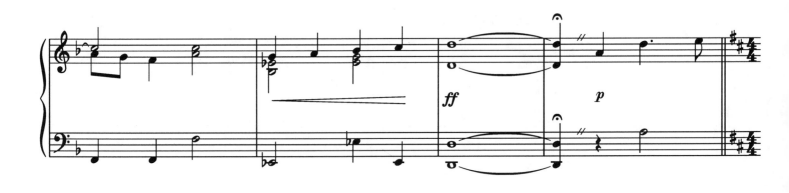

Gently (in 4)

espressivo

MEN IN BLACK

from the Columbia Pictures film MEN IN BLACK

Words and Music by WILL SMITH, PATRICE RUSHEN,
FRED WASHINGTON and TERRY McFADDEN

56

60

Men In Black. They won't let you re - mem - ber.

Rap Lyrics

1. The good guys dress in black. Remember that
   Just in case we have a face to face and make contact.
   The title held by me, M. I. B., means
   What you think you saw you did not see.

2. So don't blame me. What was dead
   Is now going black suit with the black Ray-Bans on.
   Walk a shadow, move a silence,
   Guard against extraterrestrial violence.

3. But sure we ain't on no government list.
   We straight don't exist, no names and no fingerprints.
   Saw something strange, watch your back
   'Cause you never quite know where the M. I. B.'s is at.

4. Now from the deepest of the darkest of night,
   On the horizon, bright light intercept tight.
   Cam'ra zoom on the impending doom.
   But then, like boom, black suits fill the room up.

5. With the quickest, talk with the witnesses,
   Hypnotizer, normalizer.
   Vivid memories turn to fantasies.
   Ain't no M. I. B.'s cannot believe.

6. Do what we say, that's the way we kick it.
   Yeah me, I see my noisy cricket get wicked on you.
   We're your first, last and only line of defense
   Against the worst scum of the universe.

7. So don't fear us, cheer us.
   If you ever get near us, don't jeer us.
   We're the fearless M. I. B.'s, freezing up all the flack.
   What's that stand for? Men In Black.

8. All right, check it, let me tell you this in closing.
   I know we might seem imposing.
   But trust me, if we ever show in your section,
   Believe me, it's for your own protection.

9. 'Cause we see things that you need not see,
   And we be places that you need not be.
   So go with your life, forget the Roswell crap.
   Show love to the black suit 'cause that's the Men In,
   That's the Men In.

M.I.B. MAIN THEME
from the Columbia Pictures film MEN IN BLACK

By DANNY ELFMAN

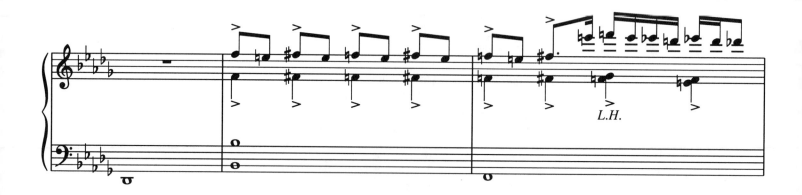

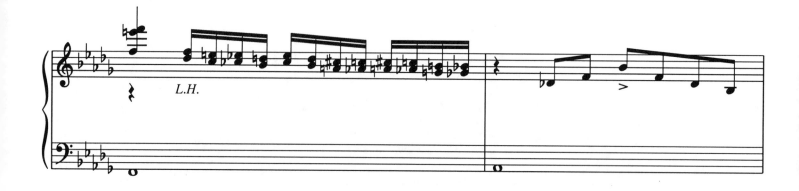

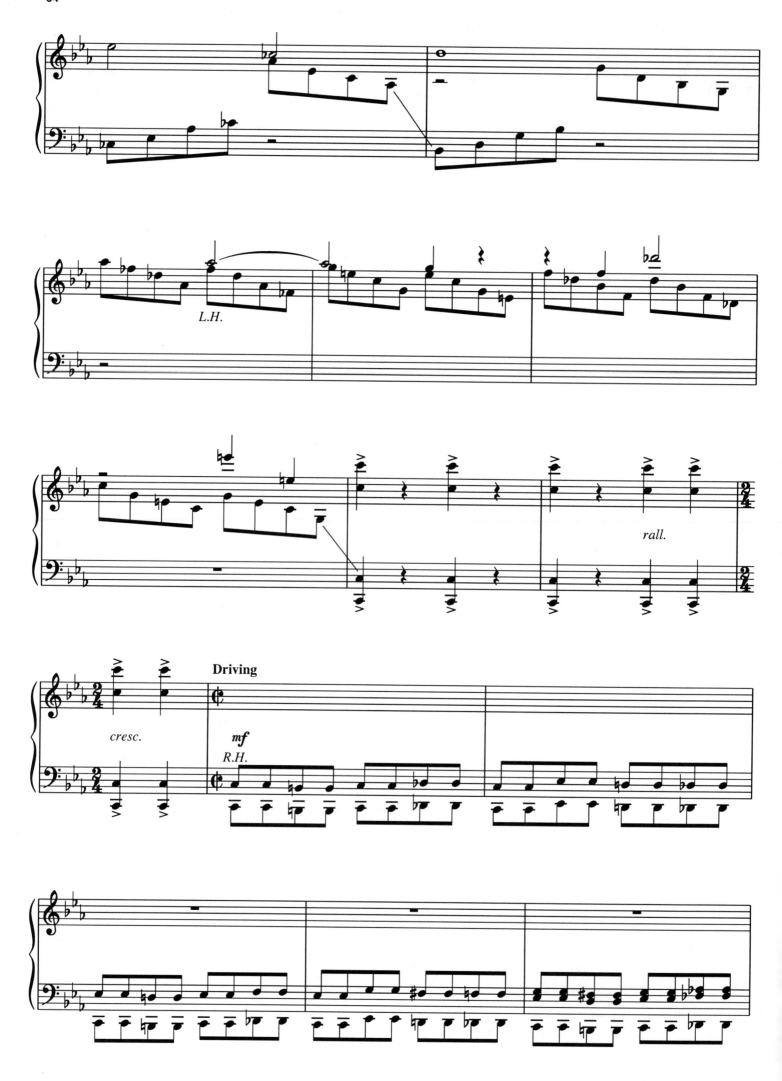

MISS MISERY
from the Miramax Motion Picture GOOD WILL HUNTING

Written by
ELLIOTT SMITH

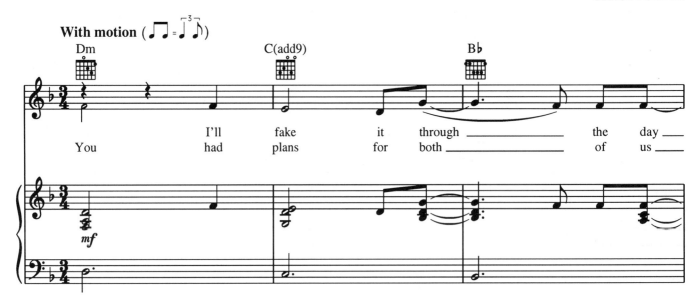

You
I'll fake it through _____ the day _____
had plans for both _____ of us _____

_____ with some help _____ from John - nie Walk - er Red. _____
that in - volved _____ a trip out of town _____

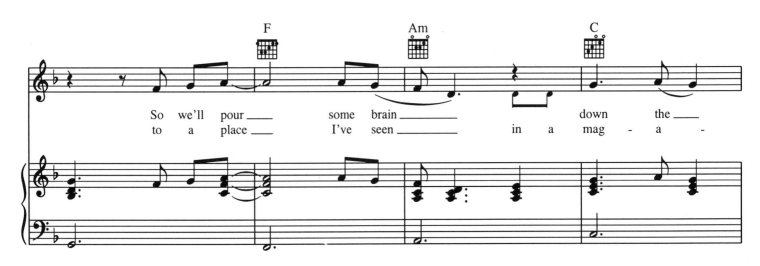

So we'll pour _____ some brain _____ down the _____
to a place _____ I've seen _____ in a mag - a -

MY HEART WILL GO ON
(Love Theme from 'Titanic')
from the Paramount and Twentieth Century Fox Motion Picture TITANIC

Music by JAMES HORNER
Lyric by WILL JENNINGS

SEVEN YEARS IN TIBET
from the Motion Picture SEVEN YEARS IN TIBET

By JOHN WILLIAMS

Broadly

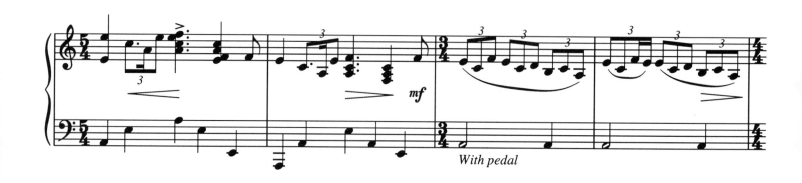

Cantabile

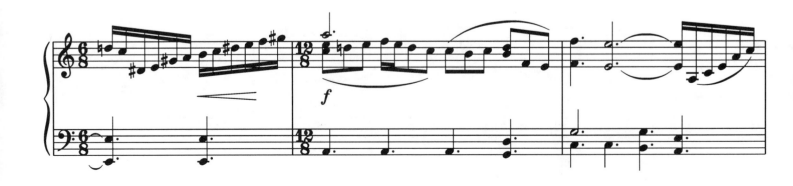

SUMMER NIGHTS
from GREASE

Lyric and Music by WARREN CASEY
and JIM JACOBS

TOMORROW NEVER DIES

from the Motion Picture TOMORROW NEVER DIES

Words and Music by SHERYL CROW
and MITCHELL FROOM

YOU MUST LOVE ME

from the Cinergi Motion Picture EVITA

Words by TIM RICE
Music by ANDREW LLOYD WEBBER

Additional Lyrics

Verse 2: *(Instrumental 8 bars)*
Why are you at my side?
How can I be any use to you now?
Give me a chance and I'll let you see how
Nothing has changed.
Deep in my heart I'm concealing
Things that I'm longing to say,
Scared to confess what I'm feeling
Frightened you'll slip away,
You must love me.

THE WAY YOU LOOK TONIGHT

featured in the Tri-Star Motion Picture MY BEST FRIEND'S WEDDING

Words by DOROTHY FIELDS
Music by JEROME KERN

THE WINGS OF THE DOVE

from the Miramax Motion Picture THE WINGS OF THE DOVE

By EDWARD SHEARMUR

Andante espressivo

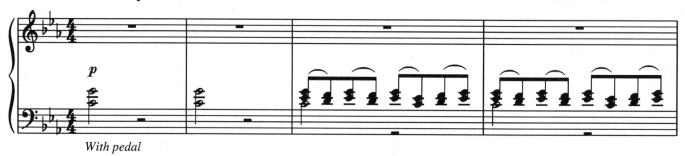

With pedal

Original key: C-sharp minor. This edition has been transposed down one half-step to be more playable.

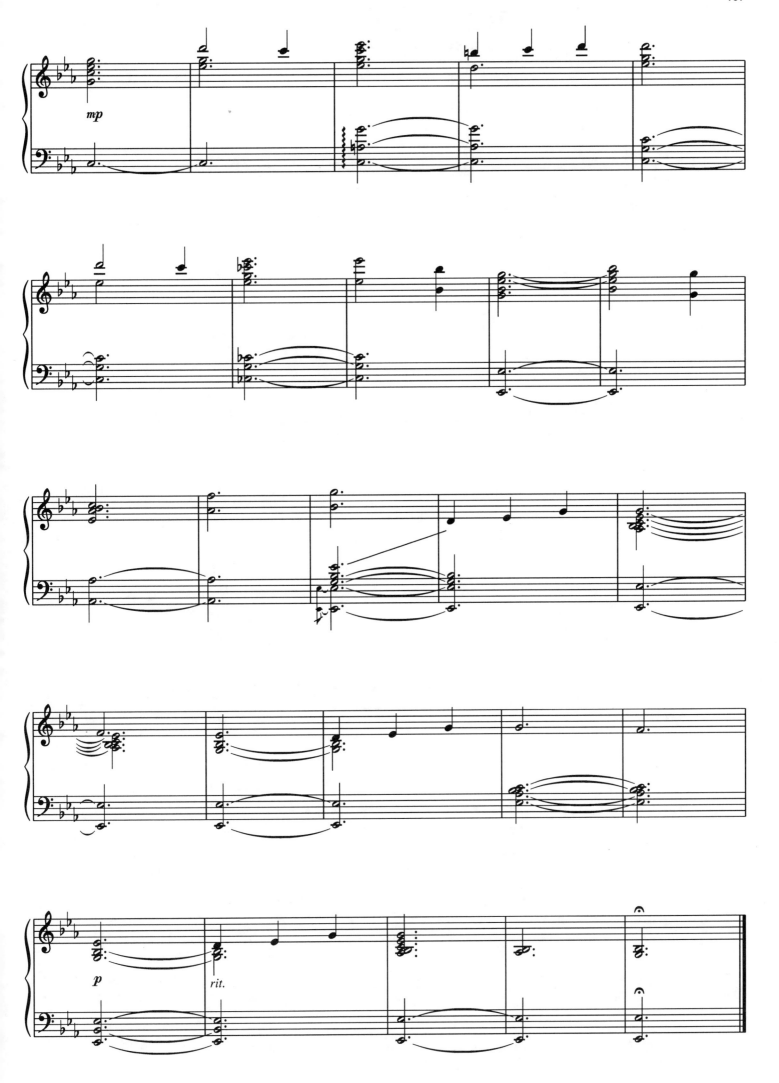

YOU SEXY THING
from THE FULL MONTY

Words and Music by
E. BROWN

I be-lieve in mir-a-cles.

Where you from, _ you sex-y thing. _ (You sex-y thing, you.)

112